MW00805150

Until
We Meet **Again**

BARBARA JEANNE FISHER

WORD ASSOCIATION PUBLISHERS
www.wordassociation.com
1.800.827.7903

Printed in the United States of America.

ISBN: 978-1-59571-996-6
Library of Congress Control Number: 2014941946

Song: "Coming Home"
Copyright © 2014. Words and music by Rick Schuler.

Published by
Word Association Publishers
205 Fifth Avenue
Tarentum, Pennsylvania 15084

www.wordassociation.com
1.800.827.7903

— ❦ —

FOR *MY DAUGHTER*

Mary Elizabeth Fisher Diaz

November 22, 1966 – November 12, 2013

There are no words in this world to explain my heart's feelings in writing this book. Having you for a daughter was one of the biggest blessings in my life.

Losing you has been heartbreaking.

CONTENTS

FOREWORD

A mother is supposed to comfort a child when he or she is so terribly sick. But you were the strong one. Your love of God, deep faith, and complete trust in Him, are life lessons meant to be shared. In a way, writing this book is a selfish act for in these pages I have a diary of all our last e-mails, hugs and kisses, talks, tears, and eternal love. But, this book would not have been possible without the rest of your family and friends, and they also crave a lasting remembrance of your love for them and the strength you brought to the challenges you faced.

Every day I wake up missing you. Sometimes I have a happy memory run through my mind, but no matter how difficult it is for me to face the day, I remember your last words to me and they give me the strength and faith to move on. My darling daughter, you were ever so right when I held your hand that last time. It was not good-bye, but ***until we meet again…***

I will always remember that last day, *leaning over my daughter knowing our time together was waning. Until then I had fought back my tears, refusing to let Mary see me cry. All at once my tears were running down my face and falling on her. She looked up at me so sad and said, "Please don't cry Mom. I'm sorry I am hurting you so much." She took my hand in hers adding, "I promise you, Mom, this is not goodbye it is only until we meet again."*

UNITIL *WE MEET* AGAIN

Mary Elizabeth, what a beautiful name! There was no discussion. My husband, Joe, and I knew before she was born if our baby was a girl our first daughter would be named after the Blessed Virgin. *Mary Elizabeth.*

Getting pregnant was a dream come true. I always wanted to get married and have children. Mary was two weeks *overdue* but she came into the world only 16 inches long and weighing a little over three pounds; she spent her first few days in an incubator. Oh, but she was alert looking over this big new world. Other new parents and their visitors would walk to the group nursery window to see their own newborn babies, but almost every one of them also stopped by the window where Mary lay alone, amazed at her size and her big brown eyes checking out this thing called life.

Because she was so tiny many people were afraid to hold her, I wasn't. I couldn't hold her enough. This little angel was my dream child.

I will never forget the day the doctor came into my room and told me "You can take your little peanut home!" Yes! We were both elated. Times were so different then for fathers. Men were not allowed to be in the hospital room when their babies were in there with their mothers. They didn't get to hold their son or daughter until they were safely home. Joe had been so disappointed. As soon as we got home he sat on the living room floor and said, "Give her to me now! She is my baby, too!"

I laughed at him and handed little Mary to him. It was love at first touch. That was the first of many times in her life that her daddy held her close to his heart, making things as right as he could.

Because Mary was so tiny her stomach could not hold much formula. I was told I could take her home if I promised to wake her up every hour and feed her a half an ounce! Looking back, I value those hours as some of the most precious of my life. I would talk to her through those late nights. Even though I knew she could not understand the words, I knew she could feel my eternal love. So often, especially in difficult times I would ask Mary if she remembered all the conversations we had during those late night hours. She always put a smile on my face when she said, "Sure, Mom, I remember every word you said back then!"

Over time we had many stories to remember about our little doll. Mary had to wear newborn size Pampers cut in half! Because she was so small we could not buy baby clothes to fit her. My grandma, who always came through in difficult times, bought 16 inch doll patterns. She set to work and made Mary several tiny sleepers and night gowns. The most beautiful was the little white baptism gown complete with a little slip and little white doll booties, the size of my thumb! Our baby was ready to receive her first sacrament in style. To this day Mary's daughter still has the booties.

Other favorite remembrances, perhaps my favorites, were from Mary's first weeks in this world. I still laugh when I think about not doing what the doctor ordered.

My doctor told me to take it easy for a while. I was told not to drive and to avoid steps. I was feeling great and a friend asked me to go shopping with her. There was only a month until Christmas so I decided to go. She did the driving, and since this was before car seats were invented, I snuggled my baby in my arms. When we got to the store I realized the baby things were on the third floor—and the store had no elevators. I stood at the bottom of three large flights of stairs. Allowing my friend to hold Mary, I started up the first flight. I couldn't wait to see the things on that third floor. I smiled to myself as I climbed without pain. What did the doctors know?

I can't remember if I bought anything that day. We returned home and I fed Mary and put her in her bassinet. I was tired after my first outing and was eager to get some rest. I drifted off to sleep deep in happy thoughts of my tiny little baby. About an hour later I felt cramping and I discovered I was hemorrhaging. I called my doctor and he told me to get to the hospital as soon as possible. What would I do with my baby?

Here is Mary Elizabeth Fisher with Grandparents, Bernard and Norma Good on her Baptism Day. She had reached four pounds and three ounces!

I called my mother. She came to my house and assured me she would take Mary to her house and watch her until I returned home. "But she is so little Mom, where can she sleep?" I was in tears not wanting to leave my baby. Mom responded without even thinking—she was the most creative person I have ever known. "I know exactly what I will do with her! She will have her own little bed in the bottom drawer of my dresser! It is small, cozy, and safe!"

I was shocked at the very idea, but after thinking about it I knew she would be in the safest place, and hopefully it would only be for a few days. Mom sensed my sadness and concerns and, as always, she tried to make me laugh. "This will work out great honey. If she gets fussy we can always shut the drawer!" I did laugh, and I knew Mary would be in the gentlest hands and be fine. I got a few things together and Joe took me to the hospital.

As I remember my stay was short and there were no complications. Doing what the doctor said really helped. I was soon back home on my nightly feeding schedule and ever so happy each time she woke me up.

Those first six weeks of Mary's life were pretty eventful. When I went back to my obstetrician for my six- week check-up, he said to me, "I thought I told you no sex until after your check up!" I agreed with him. "You did," I said. He looked me in the eye, sort of giving me a grin, "then how in the hell did you get pregnant again?" Whoops! I could not believe it, but I was so happy. Joe always told everyone that I could not keep my hands off him—but I made sure they knew the truth—he waited until I was sleeping and took advantage of me!

Mary's little sister, Julie Anne, came home from the hospital before Mary's first birthday! I was happy to have another girl so they could always play with each other. Their bond was lasting. Forty-seven years later Mary most wanted Julie to be by her side when she died.

Within the next six years we had three more children, Tammy Marie, Joseph II, and Jennifer Lynn. Mary

Mary and Julie were always together. Here they are sitting in the rocking chair dressed for bed and waiting for a good night story. 1968

seemed to be the easiest to bring up. I cannot remember her getting into trouble or talking back or running around or anything at all. She was the best of students and an avid reader. We all teased her about being born with a book in her hands. Because she was the oldest I am sure we were over protective. Everyone teased me because I would not let her cross the street alone until she was sixteen! She definitely tested life's road for her siblings. She loved her family and we all loved her.

During my children's childhood I was in the hospital a lot from different illnesses and the kids were fantastic with their dad. He would bring them to visit me every night and they learned to take care of themselves when I was absent from home. Out of need they looked out for each other, and I believe it made them stronger.

My children never complained about going to school and they were all good at getting their home-work done without too much delay. They each did very well scholastically. Mary was her class valedictorian. She received many scholarship offers and was eager to go to college. She wanted to be a college English professor. When she left home the first time I never knew it would be forever . . . I missed her so much over the years. I cherish this picture of her with her proud father, at her graduation from Findlay College with a bachelor's degree in English.

Over the next few years Mary received her M.A. in English from Illinois State University. Finally, she

Mary with Joe, May 1989.

settled in Chicago. My little girl—the one who could not cross the street alone until she was sixteen—was navigating the streets and alleys, and subways and trains, and walking endless miles to reach her goals. I was so very proud of all her achievements and the lady she had become.

From 1995-2013 she worked at the University of Chicago as a library technical assistant. While working there she met and married the love of her life.

Mary and Carlos G. Diaz were married in 1999, and later that same year their daughter, Isabella Maria, was born. Mary was totally committed to both her husband and her daughter. They were such a close knit family and enjoyed doing everything together. For most of their marriage they worked in Chicago and lived in a triplex. A few years ago, after years of cutting corners and saving, they finally moved into their dream home.

Mr. and Mrs. Carlos Diaz at their wedding Febryary 13, 1999

They were all so happy and excited. Finally, Isabella could *walk* to a school in their neighborhood. This saved Mary hours of transportation time every day. For most of her married life Mary had spent about two or three hours a day getting back and forth to work and other places.

Their new home was a dream come true for all of them. Carlos was so proud of it. He never failed to decorate the windows for the holidays, and he made beautiful centerpieces for the dining room table. Mary had waited so long for a home of her own she couldn't do enough to make it a place where they would all feel cozy, safe, and deeply loved. They shared the chores and took Isabella to see all the sites in Chicago and Disney Land. They were bonded in heart, mind, and body, and her family here in Ohio was ecstatic.

A year and a half later their near perfect world collapsed. Mary had been working long hours at the university and when she said she was not feeling well. We thought she was overtired. At the same time she started having digestive problems which were diagnosed as acid reflux. She was given some pills, but a few weeks later there was still no improvement.

In July, Mary and Carlos and Isabella came home to Ohio for a short visit. Mary was still feeling sick, but she did not complain much. She enjoyed a day out with her other sisters, visited Lakeside, and had a wonderful catch-up day. They all talked about that day the rest of the summer. On the way back to Chicago the family

Tammy, Jenny, Mary, and Julie together at Lakeside, Ohio July 29, 2013

stopped to eat and Mary got very sick. Later she said to me that she was tired of getting sick from eating.

When she got back from vacation she was in the middle of a major project at work and she was the only one who could get it done by the deadline. Fighting her intense fatigue, she returned to her doctor who changed her acid reflux medicine. Nothing seemed to help. (I found out later that her doctor had suggested she have a colonoscopy and endoscopy, but Mary wanted to finish her project first.)

With that said, may I digress just for an instant? I feel it is necessary to tell all who are reading this: If you feel something is wrong, do not wait to go to the doctor and have all the needed tests. Some doctors have told me that even if Mary had had the tests earlier it might not have made a difference because she had such a fast growing cancer. But even if it was only a small chance, there was a chance that it might have changed the ending of this story. **Please, I cannot stress too much, do not wait, always put yourself first. You only get one life**.

MARY *IN CHICAGO'S HOSPITALS*

There is so much to write about the six weeks Mary was in the hospitals in Chicago. I say hospitals as she was in two regular ones and spent the last day and a half at Rainbow Hospice.

We all knew Mary was not feeling well but she was never one to complain, so family here in Ohio never dreamed she had anything major. Furthermore, she was still seeing the doctor who kept changing her medicine to treat what was thought to be acid reflux.

On September 17, 2013 I got email from Mary that alerted me that something was very wrong:

Hi Mom,

I just wanted to let you know that Carlos is going to take me to the ER tonight. I am still having trouble keeping food down and he thinks if he takes me we might get some answers sooner rather than later as to why. He called my doctor's office and they thought it was a good idea. He is on his way now to pick me up.

I will try to let you know what the ER doctor says. You can always call later tonight for updates too. I don't imagine they will find out much right away though.

Love, Mary

I later learned that Carlos, who was afraid for Mary and knew she had been very sick for quite some time, told the ER staff that this time he wanted them to keep her until they found out what was wrong. Mary never did go back home. Later that evening Mary wrote to me:

I am still at the ER. So far they are testing my blood and urine. I am waiting right now for them to take me for a CAT scan. I will email you if I learn anything more tonight. If not, good night! Thanks for all your love and support. They mean the world to me.

Love, Mary

I responded:

If you get this I love you . . . I will be praying for you, wish I was there . . . my heart is there and my hand holding your hand.

Mom

September 18, 2013

Mary writes:

This has been a horrible day. I feel like bad news is hitting me from all directions all day. Thanks for your prayers. I prayed with the hospital chaplain today and took a communion host from some female minister. Going to start drinking that nasty laxative in a few minutes. UGH! Carlos and Isabella are coming by for a short visit soon. Isabella auditioned for the school play tonight and still has homework to do. Carlos is planning on taking tomorrow off work to be at the hospital during the tests. Why don't you wait to see what the test results are before you come, Mom? If I need surgery I am going to really need you here with me then. Love you so much, Mom

Forever, Mary

I replied:

Just thinking about you and missing you so much. I can't wait to hold you again. I hope Isabella gets to see you so she knows you are okay. This has to be really hard on Carlos, and most of all hard on you.

A mother never thinks her own kids, or adult children will suffer much medically in life . . . I almost told God today I refuse to accept this. . .I love you. I will come through the computer and tuck you in tonight.

With total love, Mom

She replied:

The doctor came by and explained both procedures to Carlos. He said the tests tomorrow won't happen until 12:30 (1:30 your time) at the earliest. I also just spoke to the cancer doctor. They need me to redo my mammogram from two days ago as things are denser than last year. And because they found slightly enlarged lymph nodes in my neck and chest, he is sending me for another CAT scan of the neck and a PET scan to identify or rule out cancer.

At this point in time we still had hope that Mary's problems could be fixed and she would come back home to us. However, she was seeing a cancer doctor, and she had enlarged lymph nodes, and I had heard enough about PET scans that my heart was screaming. I felt as if I was living in a bad dream and couldn't wake up.

The doctors proceeded to do a colonoscopy and an endoscopy. (A colonoscopy allows the doctor to look at the inner lining of your large intestine, rectum, and colon. An endoscopy allows a close examination of the esophagus, the stomach, and duodenum. During both procedures, special tools that slide through the endoscope allow the doctor to perform biopsies, stop bleeding, and remove abnormal growths for further testing).

UNTHINKABLE *NEWS*

This was close to the worst night of my life. My daughter Tammy and I were at the hospital with Carlos, and several doctors had spoken to us about Mary's surgery. We were told they had discovered a small malignant tumor in her small intestine. Their plan was to remove it, follow that with chemotherapy, and then radiation. At the time the doctors seemed optimistic and we were somewhat relieved.

I will never forget the three of us walking alongside the gurney as they pushed Mary into the operating room. I gave her a teary kiss, and she squeezed my hand and quietly told me, "I am really scared Mom." The time sitting in the waiting room making small talk with Carlos and Tammy, and wishing someone would come out and tell us how things were going, is indelibly etched in my brain. I knew any cancer was serious but at the same time I really believed we would get through this ordeal and soon life would be back to normal.

I am not sure how much later it was, but the head surgeon came out, shook our hands, then quickly pulled up a chair across from us. He started rubbing his hands together and looked as if he was afraid to speak. I am sure all of us knew when his words came they would hurt.

"I am sorry to tell you, but, I have never seen anything like this. When we operated we discovered Mary's body was full of stage IV cancer. I have never seen a forty-six year old woman like this. I am so sorry. We had no idea at all." I was in total shock. He had to be wrong. A mother isn't supposed to outlive her child. The doctor went on to say Mary's condition was critical and he could keep her alive for a bit longer, or let her die. I was in shock again. My mind and heart were totally numb.

It was difficult to grasp what he was saying. In essence it meant that he could do something to keep Mary from dying right then—but how much time or her quality of life could not be predicted. The doctor looked at us and said he would give us time to talk to make that decision. As Mary's mother it was very hard to step back and watch someone else decide whether my daughter would be alive in a few hours, or gone, but at the same time I could never have made the decision. I knew it had to be made by Carlos. I was her mother, but she was his wife, and the choice had to be his.

When the doctor left, the three of us were in shock and speechless. Then Carlos started evaluating the choices. Would it be fair to Mary to keep her alive? Were we ready to say good-bye? What if a miracle could happen and they could get her well enough to go home for a while, what if. . .

Carlos loves Mary so much. I say loves for I know his love for her will be forever. He listened to Tammy and me asking for our opinions, and he finally decided to tell the doctors to do what they could to keep her alive.

PRECIOUS TIME
IN THE HOSPITAL

The next seven weeks were totally unreal. Mary was breathing and talking but even as we tried to comfort her, it was her strength, love, and faith that gave us the courage to carry on. "One day at a time." Mary said that often and no one disagreed with her.

We learned from her oncologist that Mary was too weak to have chemo. She had to get strong before she could have any treatment. However, that was in itself unreal. She could no longer eat. She vomited up everything she swallowed. She had a feeding tube put in but even that was not working right. For weeks she had IVs for nourishment and was only allowed to have ice chips. After about the second week she announced that her teeth we falling apart from the ice.

They kept saying she had to move around and get exercise to get stronger, but she had so many tubes coming out of her from head to toe she couldn't even walk to a chair. In spite of all this, she never gave up on her wish to return to her precious home to die.

The weeks were long for all of us, but my amazing kids and husband showered Mary with love. Some of their attentions were awesome and I was so proud of my children.

Julie would travel to Chicago—a six hour drive—and give Mary a body rub, paint her fingernails, and do her hair. Mary said she loved to be spoiled! Tammy was what Mary called her best nurse. She was at Mary's side night and day and gave her ice, washed her face and hands, moved her, and gave her things she could not reach. Mary was in intensive care, and Tammy climbed on a window seat and slept there. Jenny and Joe came to see her as often as they could and that made her smile. For seven weeks Tammy was our faithful driver.

I tried to be with Mary as much as I could. Joe did not like to travel and he was in denial; he was waiting for Mary to return to her home, then he would visit her. This was a terrible spot for me to be in. He would call and want to talk to Mary, then he would fall apart and cry and my heart was shredded. I wanted to stay with my dying daughter but my husband needed me back in Ohio. I hurt for both. Common sense told me my time with my daughter was running out, and I would hopefully have a lot more time with Joe.

Mary wanted to see her father. So the other kids, ever resourceful, hopped on a Mega bus with their father and brought him to the hospital. Their reunion was tearful for sure. While Joe was there Mary started having terrible stomach pain and the doctors did another CAT scan. Immediately they discovered Mary had a chronic infection in her stomach. They inserted a tube from her belly to drain the infection out. Before her death she had five of these.

Mary never complained and all you had to do was look at her to see how much she was suffering. Julie, Tammy, Jenny and I were there a lot, and when she was having a somewhat good day we had nice talks with her, and sometimes even got a smile.

One day a couple of us were in her room chatting. She was writing on her Kindle and made the comment that she wished she had a laptop so it would be easier to write. I knew her daughter, Isabella, had one and always thought Mary did as well. She told me she always wanted one but never got it for herself!

I called Tammy in Ohio and asked her to go buy a laptop for Mary. She and Johnny went shopping and a few days later they surprised her with it. They told me Mary laughed and cried and kissed the laptop. My heart was so touched that such a little material thing could make my dying daughter smile.

Mom! Thanks so much for going to the trouble of getting me a laptop. I just really love it and it will help me get my last letters to my family done. You did not have to get it for me, but thanks again and again.

Love you always, Mary

I replied:

> *My precious daughter, you do not get it! There is no need for thanks, and it was far from trouble, I live to love and love to live and give…that is me in a nutshell. There is nothing on earth that can touch the love in my heart for you, your siblings, my grandchildren, and of course your father. This is my life and honey I am so glad you will always be beside me as well. That knowledge touches my heart in ways you can't even begin to dream of. I love you more than any words can express…Getting ready for Mass… I will offer it up for you. You are and always will be my precious little angel with a giant heart and the strength and determination to make it in the worst situations. I praise you for that. Hugs and kisses, tears and smiles, and forty-six blessed years together…*

Always, Mom

Sadly, Mary was too weak to even pick up her laptop to use it. She still used her Kindle and she wrote me so many notes that I would answer immediately. If she missed a day I went crazy wondering how she was.

RAINBOW *HOSPICE*

Two and a half days before she passed away, Mary decided to move to Rainbow Hospice. My daughter was unselfish to the end. She knew she would never get to go back home, and she decided it was time to go home to God.

For the last three days of Mary's life our entire family went to Chicago to be with her day and night. Mary was weak but totally conscious to the end. She had a chance to talk to all of her siblings and their spouses, alone and in groups. She got to talk to Joe and me together and alone. Many of these conversations were bright spots in very tough times,

Mary knew she was dying, but that didn't mean she was giving up. She organized her final days the best she could. When we first got in her room, she looked at her sister Julie, and said, "I am running out of time. I expect you to pamper me from head to toe, more than ever!" We looked at her and had to laugh.

She pointed a finger at me and said, "You are in charge of my BUCKET LIST!" I looked shocked not knowing what to expect next. I asked, "What exactly does that mean?" She went on to explain that since she had not eaten in days, and would never eat again, she wanted me to get her a caramel frappe from McDonalds's the first day, a mocha frappe the next, spaghetti the third, and if she lived longer, Chinese food. I knew she was unable to swallow a thing, and wondered what she had in mind. She said, "I just want to put these things in my mouth for a while to cherish and remember the taste." I got tears in my eyes.

I did as she said and got her the first frappe! The girls took a teaspoon of it and put it into a paper cup. Mary put her head back and ran the liquid into her mouth. She shut her eyes and swished that little bit around her mouth time and again. It made me think how much we take eating for granted. It broke my heart to see "my baby" literally dying that way. At one point she closed her eyes and leaned way back into the pillow. Not knowing how little of the frappe the girls had put in the cup, I got nervous thinking she might spill something on the bed, so I reached between the side rails and took the cup from her hands! So small, weak, and yet mighty, her other hand came up and smacked my hand, "Don't mess with my Bucket List Mom!"

On the Monday before she died I had to return to Ohio for a doctor's appointment. I hated to leave but the hospice people thought she would make it a few more days. When we were getting ready to leave, Mary kept asking for Julie. She decided she could not leave Mary and Carlos there alone. Despite other obligations, she opted to stay.

Tammy, Joseph II, and Jenny all told Mary good-bye and kissed her. Then Joe did likewise. When I went up to her bed I took her hand and told her I would be back in a day. She looked at me and told me for the very last time, "I love you so much Mom. This is not good-bye it is just until we meet again…"

We arrived home after midnight, and I called the hospice right away. They said her blood pressure was a little off but that was not abnormal and promised to call us if anything more happened. I slept with my phone. At five-thirty in the morning it rang. I knew when I heard Julie's voice that a very precious life on earth had ended. I also knew there was a new angel in heaven. Julie explained that Mary had seemed restless all night and she and Carlos had tried to make her comfortable. We thought maybe Mary wanted to be sure someone was with her.

At some point Carlos noticed Mary's labored breathing and he so nobly read her a letter he had written for that final moment. Then, around three o'clock Tuesday morning, Mary gently cried for Julie, asking her to please help her. Julie asked Mary what she needed and she said, "I want to pray." Before Julie could say anything else, she said that Mary started saying the Hail Mary in a loud steady voice. A short time later Mary breathed out her last breath. With all my heart I am so glad Carlos and Julie were with her, and just as glad that I wasn't. We talked about it and I believe Mary did not want me there when she died. I pride myself for being strong in most things, but with all my heart I believe had I been there when my Mary stopped breathing I would have totally fallen to pieces. It was as it was supposed to be.

Her father and I had already made all the plans for her funeral, but when we were doing it I am not sure we knew it would be so soon. When we picked out her casket, flowers, and grave, we knew this was for *someday*…All of a sudden it became reality. For a while even the thought of her being in heaven did not dull our pain. Looking back we both agree that it was through our love for God first, then each other and our family, and our many beautiful friends that we ourselves found a way to get beyond Mary's *someday*.

MARY'S *FUNERAL*

One weekend when Tammy and I were with alone with Mary, she handed Tammy a piece of paper and told her to take notes! Neither of us had any idea what Mary was up to.

First she told us that Carlos would eventually be cremated so she wanted to be buried in Fremont's Saint Joseph's cemetery with Joe and me. We already had our plots, so with kindness and a few changes the cemetery arranged for a third plot right by ours for our daughter. She knew her dad and I had picked out her casket and burial plot. She said time and again, "Thanks Mom for taking that worry off my mind! I thank God I will be lying beside the two people who loved me so much first."

Mary said she wanted the book *Persuasion* by Jane Austin buried with her. I wondered what was so special that she would choose this from the hundreds or thousands of books she had read. I ordered a few copies of this book and put one away for her. I still want to read it myself, but the few times I have tried I was too sad to complete it. I will do it!

She wanted her coffin lining embroidered with books and they were beautiful indeed. (She always had a book with or near her. I used to tease her telling her the worst part of her birth was when the umbilical cord got caught on the book coming out!)

She wanted a picture of herself with Carlos and Isabella, and one of her immediate family, and finally, she wanted to be buried in her wedding dress.

Mary wanted a long time wonderful friend of the family, Father Frank Kehres to officiate at her funeral. As he has been there for us for the last forty some years, he agreed. Our Parish priest, Father Ken Lill concelebrated the Mass; he too has been a precious friend and great part of our lives. The day of the funeral, to my total wonderful surprise another very special friend of ours, Father Mark Herzog showed up and the three of them conducted the most beautiful service. So much love in one place.

Mary wanted the song "Ave Maria" sung at her funeral and her twenty-two year old niece, Chelsea, not only sang like an angel but touched every heart in the church. There are no words to describe how awesome she was. Chelsea was very close to her aunt, and it took all the courage in the world to sing that song for her. I am sure my Mary will smile forever thinking of that song . . . I still do.

Mary had 650 people at her showing, and the church was packed at her funeral. Burying Mary was the hardest thing we ever had to do for one of our children. I pray to God I never have to do it again. But given the circumstances it did help to know Mary had such a beautiful funeral and it was exactly the way she wanted it.

A GLIMPSE
INTO MARY'S SOUL

The letters *from* Mary speak more clearly and more personally to the strength, courage, and wisdom of a young woman, who in the face of death, was more concerned about others than herself.

The letters *to* Mary from her family are testimony to her quiet courage and the power of her faith and caring for others.

She was a remarkable woman, and it did not go unnoticed by those she cared for. Here is a sampling of the letters sent and received.

LOVING
CORRESPONDENCE

Mom,

They are trying to figure out why my white blood cell count is high. I will let you know the results when I find out. I can't see it being anything serious as I have had a quiet night and the test was done hours ago.

I am not afraid of death Mom. I don't want to drag out the suffering for all concerned. I found my true love & have spent 14 years with my beautiful, creative, and quirky child. I am blessed and I am at peace. If it is my time to go, I embrace it willingly with acceptance and love. I look forward to seeing Evan again, as well as all my grandparents. And when the rest of you follow me, I will be waiting for you with open arms. I love all of you so much. Death should bring us closer together, not tear us apart.

I know when my time comes, you will give me a beautiful send off just like you did Grandma Fisher. That was the most beautiful funeral service I ever attended and it brought me back to God.

I just thought of two of my favorite religious songs for the service, they are "Ave Maria" and "On Eagle's Wings.

I know I am going to heaven a lot earlier than any of us thought, but life has been so good to me, and I know in my heart we will all be together again.

Mom, this is only until we meet again.
Love, Mary

Mom,
The most beautiful thing in my entire life was having my mom holding and rubbing my hand when I was dying. I love you so much, Mom.

Always, Mary

P.S. I also love the beautiful prayer shawl you got me Mom. I always wrap it around my shoulders and pretend it is you hugging me.

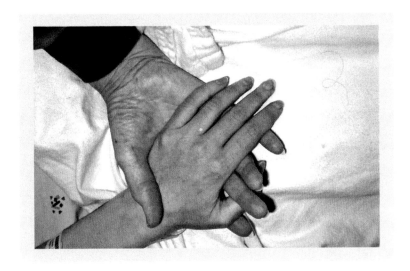

— ❦ —

October 5, 2013

My dearest Isabella,

I have asked your dad to give you this letter after my death. First of all, I know your feelings are going to be all confused when I go. Part of you will be sad and lonely and will never stop missing me. Don't forget that even though I am no longer with you in person, I will always be in your heart. You will have your letters from me, my photo books and photos, and your memory of our times together to keep me alive.

I want you to think of me as your guardian angel watching you from above. Whenever you need to talk to me I will be there listening and loving you so very much.

I also know that part of you will be relieved that my suffering is over. That is okay too and a normal way to feel. I will be at peace with God and his angels. I look forward to seeing little Evan again. And I will be so happy to see all my grandparents again, especially my grandmas as I was closest to them. Plus, many, many years from now, when it is your time to join me, I will be waiting for you; my arms open wide in a big hug.

There are three things I want to ask of you now that I am gone.

First of all, look out for your dad and always stay close to him. He is the best of husbands and dads and deserves all the love and loyalty you can give him. This doesn't mean you cannot lead separate lives but rather that you make an effort to stay close and include him in your life once you marry and have your own kids. I don't want him to end up a lonely bitter old man, that is why I would be happy to see him remarry. He has had a lot of suffering in his life and deserves to be happy.

Second, please keep in touch with my family in Ohio. I love them all so much and it would make me so very happy to know that you love them too. They will help you grieve and can help you laugh again with some funny "Mary stories" from my childhood.

Finally, my darling, I hope that this experience will not turn you bitter and negative against the world, but rather make you into a stronger, more sympathetic, and wiser woman. I will be the first to tell you that cancer has always been one of my strongest fears. However, one positive result of my cancer has been a tremendous outpouring of love from family, friends, coworkers, and most especially strangers. I have heard story after story from others about how their suffering has changed their lives for the better and allowed them to reach out and help others. I think the key is to get past feeling sorry for yourself and seeing that positive things can result from adversity. Your dad told me that death is not evil and he is right. I think what I am trying to say is try not to see yourself as a victim but rather as a young woman who was very lucky to have had fourteen plus years to spend with her loving mother. This experience will show you who really loves you and that is a wonderful thing to know. The most important lesson I want you to take away from this experience is how precious each day is and that you should never take it for granted.

You will get past this Isabella, although things will never quite be the same again. You are stronger than you know. Plus you have your dad, his family, and my family to talk to. It is very important to share your feelings and work your way through them. Don't be ashamed to cry and show your feelings. Big girls do cry and it will make you feel better.

I am signing off now, but I want you to know that in some way I will always be there for you in your heart or watching you from above.

Love eternally, Mom

— ☺ —

My dearest eighth grader,

I think of you with tears in my eyes, not knowing if I will live long enough to see you on this long awaited happy day. Either way my heart is bursting with pride to have such a talented hard working daughter like you. I have watched you over the years as you blossomed from preschooler and grew and matured into an independent, creative, humorous, intelligent 8th grader. I hurt when you were hurt by bullies, cheered your many accomplishments especially your beautiful art work, your very creative writing, and your outstanding grades. Your sorrows were my sorrows; your joys my happiness.

As you finish your childhood and move into high school, I encourage you to continue your hard work, and success will follow in life, both in high school and college.

Also my dearest Isabella, I urge you to savor each day to the best of your ability because, as we have seen, tomorrow is guaranteed to no one.

Please give your dad a hug and kiss from me and have him do the same for you. And always remember that in one way or another I will always be at your side and in your heart to guide you no matter where you choose to go in life.

Love always, Mom

— ❧ —

LIFE LESSONS
FROM MARY TO ISABELLA

October 13, 2013

Here is the accumulation of 46 years of thoughts. It will be at random, but here are the things I would most like you to know as you face life; life lessons as it were…

God and Religion - *At times when you seem most alone and doubt the existence of God, this is the time you need to make a leap of faith and believe in the existence of God. If you look closely enough you will see him in the beauty of nature and the kindness of strangers and in the warmth and love of your own family.*

Family First - *Family should always come first. They do the most for you and their love and loyalty should be rewarded. Friends and lovers come and go but family is forever. That is why you should always try to love and respect and appreciate the members of your own home first. A peaceful harmonious home life is the best foundation for a happy life.*

Life is not fair, but it really is - *As you go through life you may often think that others have it easier than you or they are luckier than you. Once you get to know most people, you will see that everyone has their own sort of sorrow. Envy of others only hurts you. Forgiveness and peace and moving on with a positive attitude will result in a healthier stronger you.*

It is better to be kind than to be always right - *Think twice before wounding people unnecessarily with hurtful words. You may triumph in the moment but lose a longtime friend.*

Relationships - *Actions speak louder than words. Other people should not be able to use the words I love you as an excuse to be hurtful to you. If they really love you, they will treat you with the respect and dignity that you deserve. Of course, you will hurt and be hurt by the people you love, but I'm sorry should mean I will try not to hurt you again.*

Money - *Money, its use and its priority is one of the things you must agree on for a happy relationship. A spender is usually not happy married to a saver. As for me, where money is concerned, I think the happiest people are those who choose the middle ground; spend some and save some. Extreme saving or spending seems to result in unhappiness.*

Health – *Health is one of life's greatest priorities. If you are good to your body, it will be good to you.*

Children – *Children are one of life's greatest joys. Not only are they a part of you born again, they bring back the joy of life as everything is new and fresh when you see it through their eyes.*

Greatest Gift – *The greatest gift is peace of mind. Try to love yourself for who you are. Try to find the joy in the smallest daily routines of life. Life is mostly a series of everyday moments meant to be savored* *rather than one big happy event that can't live up to our expectations.*

Memories - *Even though you may lose someone you love through death, they can still live on in your heart as long as you carry their memory there. Remember our times together both happy and sad and I shall always be with you, beside you to guide you eternally.*

Love Always, Mom

Mary and Isabella together on a beautiful day

— ❦ —

Dear Dad,

I love you so much. You are my first hero and one of the wisest men I know. Thank you for all your years of hard work on my behalf. You fed me, clothed me, put a roof over my head, and sacrificed even further to send me to a good Catholic school. I want to let you know how much I appreciate all that and always will.

You taught me many valuable life lessons, both by words and example. I remember when I was a little girl you told me to always do my best or I would have to do it a second time. You helped me come to terms with Grandma Fisher's death when you said you missed her but wouldn't want her back the way she was.

My greatest memory of you has been the way you stood by Mom through many rough years of medical problems. I always wanted a husband that would show the same loyalty towards me and I believe I found him in Carlos. As a husband and a dad, I admire you more than you will ever know. Another thing I love about you Dad is your honesty. You tell it like it is and you are not afraid to be yourself. I am so lucky to have known you and had you for a father.

Finally, thanks for helping make my childhood a happy one. You always made me laugh, whether it was dressing up as Santa and trying to sing or inventing your own words. You helped make my childhood a little more fun. After I am gone, please comfort Mom as best you can. I know this is really hard on both of you, but remember I am in a better happier place now. You will miss me but you wouldn't really want me back the way I was. Please stay close with Carlos and Isabella. I want them to love you as much as I do.

I want to thank you for buying my cemetery plot so that I can lie next to you and Mom. That was one of the most beautiful gifts I have ever received. It is a great comfort to me to know that I won't be alone but next to two of the dearest people on earth to me. One day Dad, we will meet again and I want to take that long beautiful bike ride with you. Until then, carry me in your heart and remember I will always be with you in the memories of all the happy times we shared together.

Love always, Your daughter, Mary

LETTERS TO MARY
FROM HER
CHERISHED FAMILY

My Darling Little Mary,

From day one you were so little and precious but you showed the world you could stay awake and look all around you to see your new world. I was never afraid to hold you but many, many people were! You were a sign that there is a God and He had a part in creating you. You made me a mother and that had always been one of my lifetime dreams.

Over the years you were the easiest to bring up. I cannot remember you getting into trouble or talking back or running around or anything at all. I know they teased me because I would not let you cross the street until you were sixteen! You were the best of students and an avid reader. You loved your family and we all loved you.

When you left home the first time I never knew it would be forever . . . I have missed you so much over the years. I still love the picture of you and dad at Findlay when you graduated. One college, another town, you moved and moved. You ran along streets, took subways, and trains, and walked miles to reach your goals. You can be very proud of all your achievements and the lady you became (mostly on your own). And then, when you were praying to Saint Theresa to find a husband, Carlos came over with the rose, a sign that the prayer had been answered . . . what a miracle that was!

You had your little girl who is slowly become a woman. Both you and Carlos have done a wonderful job. All the time you spent with Isabella and Carlos are a permanent part of their lives . . . the best of times for them.

I loved when you came home and we got a day or two by ourselves. I wish there had been more. I am glad we had email, and our phone calls. I loved the holidays when you were home longer.

I feel so empty right now. . . I wish I was there with you. I wish I could take your heart and hand in mine and assure you that your future will be far more beautiful than anything either of us have ever dreamed of . . .no pain, no fear, no sadness, or grief, all happiness with people you knew before who loved you with all their hearts. And the Blessed Virgin ... Wow. Oh, Mary that will be so great, trust me on that. I so look forward to seeing her someday.

Mary, listen to me, our bodies may die but our hearts and souls live on. Love is eternal, and even when people leave us, the love is there forever and ever I know that for a fact. Love is forever, and forever never ends.

I love you more than any words can express. If it were possible I would change places with you. This is all wrong. I am mad at life and questioning God for the first time in my life ...

I promise you after you are gone that I will love and care for Carlos and Isabella. I will do all I can to help her follow her heart's dreams. I will also make sure you are always a part of her life. I promise.

Got to get to bed. This is almost a book. Good night my beautiful daughter. I am going to sleep with your picture tonight and hold you close to my heart ... your heart will always be in my heart.

Love, Mom

— ⌢ —

Dear Mary,

My first memory of you was your being so small at birth. The other babies at the hospital were all sleeping, but you were awake and looking around at the Big World! I later realized you were planning your direction in life. Already you were trying to locate a book and get your nose in it! This love of reading gave you a great amount of knowledge and pleasure through your entirely too short life.

You were such an easy going and quiet child, a great example to your sisters and brother. I remember you asking many, many questions. From the time you started kindergarten you began to excel which continued throughout your life. Your mom and I often laugh when we remember you coming home from school and telling us you learned all about Abe Linconham!

Because you were off to college shortly after high school, and living and working out of state, the next twenty-eight years seem like a fast moving blur. Our relationship was limited to phone conversations and a few visits each year. I wonder if any of us took the time to tell you how badly we missed you.

We all knew you were a dynamic person, but only after seeing the video your co-workers at the university library made for your memorial service, did we fully realized how amazing and what a respected person you were. All the employees stressed how they could always lean on you, and know you would keep the place going smoothly day to day.

It was so great to see the great pride you and Carlos took in raising Isabella to be the fine young lady she is today. It was also so wonderful to watch the joy you and Carlos had in finally having your own home.

There is no doubt that in your too short life you made our world a much better place. Life here is often lonely without you. We do find peace in knowing we will see you again in the next life! I hope there are bicycles in heaven so we can finally take that beautiful long awaited ride together . . . maybe even more than one!

Until we meet again, hold down the fort in heaven. As much as I miss you, I am in no hurry to get there. With forever love, "Your Favorite Dad!

— ❦ —

IT'S NOT EASY *LETTING GO*

Growing up I always felt the need to look after Mary, making sure she was well cared for and safe from harm. Even though she was my older sister—though by less than a year—she always seemed more vulnerable to me. Mary would make life interesting for me by getting herself into all sorts of silly little situations. If there were a single puddle within a hundred yard radius, Mary would not only find it, but somehow manage to step in it.

Her driving skills were not one of her better attributes. I recall one time, as we were driving down the highway, I questioned why she was driving so slowly. Come to find out, she had mistakenly thought the Route 20 sign was the speed limit. Once, when we were grocery shopping together, I fell ill and was on the verge of fainting. Mary and I laughed about who would be the safer of the two to drive us the few blocks to home. I believe I allowed Mary behind the wheel since it was such a short distance.

It is not because she was not bright, because Mary was very smart. I believe, looking back, she just always had her head in a cloud and her nose in a book. She loved her books as they would take her to the many make believe worlds she came to love.

There were many days in the summer when my mother felt my siblings and I should be out playing in the sunshine. Mary and I would make mud pies and salads out of grass and dandelions or play cops and robbers. However, there were many days I would sneak in through the basement window to get out of the heat, only to find Mary already lying on the couch well into her favorite mystery novel.

My parents raised us five kids in a relatively small house. So, needless to say, there was not much elbow room and there was often quite a bit of sibling rivalry. Mary was not perfect, but I cannot remember her ever getting in any of the rough and tumble quarrels like the other four of us. However, I recall an instance where Mary happened to be in the wrong place at the wrong time and took a blow to the mouth as I ducked from my brother's fury. Although I was relieved to have dodged the punch, I felt bad for innocent Mary and her swollen lip. For the most part, Mary avoided controversy. She generally went with the flow and didn't get rowdy like the rest of us.

That is until her final, precious, few weeks here on earth. My quiet, reserved Mary showed me a side of her I had long forgotten. Although gracious in every way, Mary laid clear expectations for each of us. My duties consisted of pampering her through hand and foot massages, facials and pedicures. Her ordering me around reminded me of how she used to put me in my place when we were younger. It was then I remembered why Mary did not have to get rowdy to prove her point. When Mary and I would get in a wrestling match or disagreement, there would be no doubt in my mind that I could put little Mary in her place. However, all she had to do was dig her nails into my arm to prove her point. Mary was not weak; she just chose to practice quiet strength.

One night, after a couple of weeks without food, a nurse came into her room and offered her a small container of apple juice. I watched Mary light up as she savored a couple of sips from her straw. One would have thought they had brought her liquid gold. I was reminded of what is important in life and how often we take for granted the seemingly unimportant things. Mary's life became all about simple pleasures. She was ecstatic when her husband and I rigged up a plastic tub with a garbage bag and washed her hair for the first time in weeks. She found comfort in having clean hair, and did not mind the extra attention.

One night I asked Mary if I could spend the night at the hospital with her. I wanted to spend every minute

I possibly could with her. Secretly, I wanted to learn as much about Mary as I could. I felt I needed to connect with her as deeply as possible so when she passed I would have more to hang onto. It was painful even anticipating the loss of Mary from my life. We did not get much sleep, but we shared a bittersweet evening. We talked about a number of things.

One of her biggest regrets was that she would never get to hold her grandbabies. We made a pact that night. When she passed she would watch over my baby son, Evan, who would greet her in heaven. In exchange, I would try hard to be the best grandmother to Mary's future grandbabies. Whoever thought we would be making such compromises at this time in our lives. I did sneak a little request in that she be on the lookout for my future husband…from her heavenly perspective. She teased me back saying I may have to settle for pennies.

During one of our conversations, I told Mary how proud I was of her for the way she was handling her situation. She looked at me and said "I do not have a choice." I disagreed with her. Mary handled her illness with the same grace she displayed in her daily life. She never asked why it had to happen to her. I saw tears, but she never screamed, ranted and raved, or threw things. She consistently thanked her caregivers every time they walked in and induced more pain. She was graceful every step of the way. The thought of losing Mary hurt so much that I would have traded her places and told her so. She reminded me that this was her destiny, not mine.

Mary hated what was happening to her body, but she chose to share the good, bad, and the ugly with her family. I know it must have been hard for her as she felt she was losing her dignity by her ravaged body. She had to endure things and we witnessed things that nobody should ever have to undergo. However, I never saw Mary more beautiful inside and out. I think this is why I felt she needed to be pampered as much and I needed to be the one doing it. I felt the need to assure her that no matter how much her disease ravaged her little body, she was still the beautiful human being I saw her to be. I loved that my touch brought her so much comfort. Her trust in me to love her as she was and to still recognize her beauty was a gift to me. Mary is my hero.

On Sunday, two days before Mary passed away, we moved her to a hospice facility. Our entire family came from out of town to be with her and to say our good-byes. Due to outstanding obligations, we had planned to head back home to Fremont the following morning, with some of us promising to be back on the weekend. I was coming back to celebrate our last birthday together, but I didn't want to leave Mary now. I was discussing with Mary's husband, Carlos, my work and school schedule.

I had a class the following night and missing it would require several hours of extra work added to my already demanding schedule. However, Mary made my decision to stay easy. All she had to say was "Julie, I want you to stay." At that moment, nothing else mattered. Of course, she reminded me that I needed to start pampering her right away as she had little time left.

Since the onset of her illness I had felt an overwhelming sense of helplessness. Mary was slowly dying and there was not a damn thing I could do about it. I knew I had to stay strong for Mary even though I wasn't feeling it on the inside. Mary shared with me some of her fears concerning the final decline of her body. I couldn't help her get well, but I was determined to make her final moments comfortable and address her concerns with the appropriate caregivers.

My last day with Mary was her final gift to me. I felt honored that she chose me to serve her. She had a few special visitors that sat quietly and talked with me about Mary and shared stories while Mary listened. That day, I realized how much Mary was loved and respected by her friends and co-workers. Throughout the day I sat by Mary's bedside and gratefully catered to her every need. At first it was about every 15-20 minutes that I would feed her some ice chips, reposition her, or perform other tasks to keep her comfortable. At one point, she took my hand and looked me in the eye and then thanked me for loving her as much as I did. I told her she made it easy to love her.

As the day went on Mary demanded more attention and more close monitoring. Whenever I left the room, even for the slightest amount of time, Mary would find a reason to call me right back to her. I believe she had learned over the years that I would always have her back.

Although Mary's last few months were hell, her death was peaceful. There came a point when I knew there was no turning back. I had now spent 16 plus hours by Mary's bedside and could see she was slowly declining. Her husband, Carlos, had been working on a letter to read to Mary. I suggested if he wanted Mary to hear it, then now would be a good time. I left the room to give them their privacy. His letter brought a smile to Mary's face. From that point on Mary continued to grow more restless, almost in a panic. She was asking for the same things over and over, more out of habit than a real need. I took her hands in mine and we prayed the Hail Mary together. She vocalized every single word loud and clear and I could feel the peace she drew from the words. The nurses gave her a bit of medicine to make her more comfortable and to relieve some of her anxiety. Carlos and I tried to get a little rest while Mary was resting as it had been a very long day.

A few short hours later Carlos came to me in the dark and said he thought Mary had passed away. I went over to her side and switched on the light. My Mary was gone. Seeing Mary, my heart instantly fell to my feet. Carlos had heard her take her last breaths, but didn't want to wake me for fear I would try to stop her from leaving me. I still deal with the guilt of having fallen asleep on Mary when she needed me the most. If I had just stayed awake a few more hours. Carlos was right; I do not know that I would have been able to willingly let Mary go.

Looking back at all the events that transpired prior to Mary's passing, I am convinced that Mary's quiet strength is what got many of us through this difficult situation. Although she had lost total control of what was happening to her physically, she remained in control of her destiny up until her final breath. I firmly believe Mary left us early that Tuesday morning with a purpose in mind. I chose to stay with her to help with her passing, while she made sure I was still able to make it to class later that evening, five hours away. She had a knack for serving others up to the end. I realized the Mary I tried so hard to look after all my life quietly had my back the entire time.

Love you always, Ju
(Julie)

— 🙂 —

Dear Mary,

Remember our cats named Frank and George? We didn't like George because he was orange! You came up to me one day and said "I found this book of witchcraft at the library. It has spells in it to get rid of unwanted things!" We decided to gather up our rose petals, library book, and of course, George, and head to the front porch. We sprinkled the rose petals on poor George's head, and said our little spell. Ironically, George disappeared. To this day, I am still confused!

You loved to read. I remember the time that I saw you reading an encyclopedia. (They were, of course, labeled A-B, C-D, etc.) Thinking that you were looking up something in particular, I asked you what you what it was, and you told me you were going to read the entire set. I guess maybe that is how you became valedictorian of your class.

When I think of you in our childhood years, a smile comes to my face every single time. You had nicknames like "string bean," and "Florence"!!! We all had a lovely nickname...and we all hated them!

Looking back, I have an image of you and Joe wrestling. You were the only one of us that was brave enough to take him on…and you always had the attitude that YOU were going to win. However, you were always giggling so hard while wrestling, that you were soon pinned to the ground, yelling for help!

Remember Dad and I taking you to college? You were so nervous and excited! After our hugs goodbye, Dad and I headed back home. It wasn't until we were halfway home that we realized you never took your belongings out of the back seat of the car. So, of course, we had to turn around and head back.

You always believed that no one has an easy life. You lived your life honestly—you were who you were. You were a loving mother and wife. You always respected everyone, and everything, and you were a very hard worker at everything you did.

I have been so extremely blessed to have had you in my life. I have loved being your sister, for NOT ENOUGH years, and I have learned a lot from you over the years… especially at the end. I was lucky to be able to spend a good part of the last seven weeks of your life with you. We had some laughs, and a lot more tears, many "I love you" and good byes, and on two different occasions, you gave me a look that said "everything will be okay." One more example of you telling me that I will be okay, until we meet again. I will love and miss you every single day.

Tammy, your favorite sister!

Mary was a special person. She was quiet but strong. She was kind hearted and selfless. She was content with little. She seemed to be a model mother and wife. I could never figure out how this little lady was able to move to a big town like Chicago, when I, being a big man, was afraid to visit.

I think the most special time I ever spent with Mary was during a visit several years ago to Chicago. After we arrived my wife and kids wanted to see the town, so Carlos took them out. The last thing I wanted to do was get back in a car after our long drive.

Mary and I ordered pizza for delivery. We dug through old photos, and she showed me a family tree. We talked for hours. I think we might have finished watching a movie together. The next morning I remember Mary making homemade pancakes. She was so methodical about it. I reached the end of my patience and had to take over. Besides, she was making about two inch diameter pancakes, instead of the pan-sized ones I was accustomed to.

I am so proud of the way Mary finished her life. Again, she showed great strength in the way she faced adversity. She made a plan. She wrote letters to family. She gave instruction to her daughter and husband on how to proceed in her absence. Again selfless, when many others might have been lying around feeling bitter.

I never realized my feelings for my sister. I am very much aware of them now as I can barely get through writing this. Mary's passing has drawn our family together. I really appreciate all of them much more. I am seeing encouraging signs from Isabella, Mary's daughter. She finally talked to me. Carlos was a gentleman from day one and still is. May God bless you, Mary.

Your favorite (only) brother, Joe

— 🙢 —

Dear Mary,

My heart has been so sad and empty since our final good-bye. I believe in my heart that you are in a much happier place. I miss you with all my heart every minute of every day. I am sad wishing we could have been closer sisters and friends. With your living so far away, both of us working and raising families, time passed so quickly. I realize now that if either one of us knew our time together was ending so quickly we would have made the time to be together more. I realize that the past cannot be changed but we can all learn from the mistakes we make in life.

I am so proud of having you for a sister, you were always so gentle and kind. Even in the most difficult times always seemed to "do the right thing." You touched so many lives by being the person you were. I know now why they pray, "Hail Mary full of grace" as that was the way you lived your life. And you left us, in the end, praying to the Virgin Mary.

You brought our family even closer together and helped all of us realize what is most important in our lives. My twelve -year- old daughter told me that "life is too short to always be sad. Even when something hurts you 'so much,' you have to move on. You have to look at the bright side of everything even if it is dark outside. Every day you live you are one day closer to Aunt Mary."

Mary, thank you for all the precious things you taught me in your life, and especially in the way you died. Everyone knows you are in heaven watching over us. I love you and miss you every day. With love until we meet again,

Your youngest sister, Jenny

ISABELLA MARIA DIAZ
A TRIBUTE TO HER MOTHER

With great love and courage Isabella wrote and read this at her mother's wake.

> Mary was one unforgettable woman who walked into our lives. All of us gather here today to commemorate Mary. She had a wonderful personality.

> Mary had tenderness and integrity. She had a unique talent of being able to get along with

everyone. Mary wanted to make friends, not enemies, and she was capable of that. She was able to accept anyone for who they were and was a fantastic friend to all of us. Mary made peace instead of war.

Empathetic. She was empathetic. She could put herself in other peoples' shoes and because of that, she never wanted to hurt anyone's feelings. She cheered people up when they were feeling down and would be there for you through thick and thin.

Mary taught me how to accept people. She told me not to judge people or make fun of them for their physical appearance. Personalities should be judged instead.

You never realize how good something is until it is gone. That is how it was with my mom. But I am thankful for getting to know her for fourteen years of my life. Mary was a great mom and role model. I want to grow up to be like her someday.

I will mourn for her death. But no matter how bumpy the road gets, I will still continue on. I will always think "What would she want me to do?" when it comes to making decisions. I can and will achieve success. I will become a better person. I will become independent like her.

Mary will always be remembered and never forgotten. And remember everyone, do as my friend says "stay strong."

Lovers and Best Friends

A LOVING TRIBUTE
TO MARY
FROM HER DEVOTED HUSBAND, CARLOS

AN ANGEL *NAMED MARY*

Mary was the epitome of what it means to be a lady. She was polite, wholesome, gentle, well mannered, graceful, kind, and proud but yet humble. She took pride in the simple yet most important things in life; responsibility, honesty, loyalty, trustworthiness, caring, and respect for all. I believe that she left this world, satisfied with what she left behind; a loving family that demonstrated those virtues.

Mary wasn't one to seek attention. In a large gathering, she was the quiet mouse in the corner. However, the people who took the time to chat with her always came away feeling better for it. Once you got to know Mary, you knew she was a special person, someone with whom you could be yourself, without any fears of being judged. Her kindness was genuine, making one feel safe and cared for. That was Mary's charm. *Just like an angel.*

Mary was part of a rare breed. She looked at the good that people had to offer rather than the bad. There were some who took advantage of her kindness, but somehow this did not change the way she wanted to look at people. I couldn't really understand it myself, but this was Mary. *Just like an angel.*

Mary was a reservoir of untapped potential. If she so desired, she could have become a successful writer. However, Mary had no interest in achieving fame and fortune, for it facilitates the destruction of marriages and families. Regretfully, I believe that the world lost out on a great talent. However, I take solace in the fact that Mary was happiest living a simple life. *Just like an angel.*

Mary was often overlooked, underappreciated, and taken for granted. It often happens to those who prefer to remain in the background. It often bothered me, and I would tell her to be more selfish. But this was not in her nature. She felt awkward placing herself before others. She would much rather keep the peace than battle for selfish interests. *Just like an angel.*

Mary had a quiet wisdom about her. I only became aware of it near the end of her life. It was never more evident than in her "Life Lessons" letter to her daughter Isabella. It brought tears to my eyes and to the eyes of all my coworkers with whom I shared it. I never knew she had such wisdom. It was the type of wisdom that can be best described as profound and heavenly. *The wisdom of an angel.*

Mary's kind nature and manners can be easily viewed as a sign of weakness. I for one was guilty of such thinking. However, I was proven very wrong. Mary had to suffer a series of incredibly devastating news concerning her health, each one progressively worse. Yet somehow she amazed me, my daughter, and the rest of her family. No matter how cruel and unfair her fate had become, she accepted it bravely and blamed no one for it. To the end, she was always thinking of others before herself. She was determined to leave her family in good order and after doing so, sacrificed herself so as to spare them any more grief. It was one of the bravest acts I have ever seen. I wouldn't have expected anything less from my Angel.

A TRIBUTE AND FOND
REMEMBRANCE
FROM RICK SCHULER

I met Mary and all of Joe and Barbara Fisher's children and grandchildren at a little concert I performed at their cabin in the late fall of 2012. Mary, her sweet little daughter, Isabella, and her husband, Carlos, were there with everyone else. I think it was the next evening during one of the shows I did at the Strand in Fremont, Ohio that Isabella spilled her drink on a friend of the family. She was so upset that I dedicated a song to the little doll…

Barbara and her family stayed close to me the following year. We stayed in touch by email and phone. One of the highlights of our friendship was when I performed at the Hershey Theme Park. I invited Barbara and Joe to come to my concert. We saw a lot of each other. We ate together, talked, laughed and even cried a few times. Many of my best friends, and even my mother was there for this special concert and it was a wonderful touching time for all of us.

Last November Barbara wrote and told me that her oldest daughter Mary was in a Chicago hospital for tests and things did not look good. As weeks past she kept me updated on Mary's condition. Things were getting worse each time we talked. I prayed very hard for Mary and her family. In truth, they had become an extended part of my own family.

During one of our late October phone calls, Barbara mentioned that Mary had told her that John Denver was always one of her favorite singers. When she was growing up they always went to John's concerts. Then Mary added, "I love to hear Rick singing all of Johnny Denver's songs, Mom! He sounds just like John did or even better!" Then Mary went on to tell Barbara that she loved the songs that I wrote myself best, and she said she loved "Coming Home" best of all. "I just love that song, Mom. It is all about how I feel right now."

Without hesitation I told her I was going to call Mary right away and sing that song to her.

The first time I called she was in too much pain to speak. But about two weeks before she died, we did get the opportunity. It was magical!

I was shocked. When Mary answered the phone, her voice was unbelievably strong and I told her she sounded amazing! We chatted briefly and then I sang "Coming Home" for her and we both cried. It was like time was standing still and I was sharing a brief and holy moment with a woman facing her death and yet not afraid. She was sweet, strong, brave, and prepared to meet her Lord Jesus. I was so moved by the tone of her voice which communicated so much composure and strength and resolve...

We talked of family and even laughed about some things that I can't quite remember. It was such a beautiful conversation. She told me how much she loved my song and she watched the YouTube version of it as well. She also downloaded the song and told me she liked it better than any John Denver song! I cried. I still cry when I remember this, even now... especially now. Only two weeks later Mary courageously "went home" to a place where all her fear and suffering were over forever.

Allow me to explain…

You see, I grew up from the age of 13 being compared to John Denver and have been compared to him my entire life. I had to wear glasses at that age and I was as depressed about it as teenage kids get about these things. I was a skinny, shy, blue eyed, blonde haired kid with terrible myopic eyesight and my only talent was that I could play the clarinet (which I hated) and read music (which hadn't gone very far into my heart yet). I always thought I would play the guitar someday. Then one evening I saw a movie on television called *Sunshine* and for the first time, I heard the song "Sunshine On My Shoulders." It was sung by an actor in the movie and not John Denver, but I fell in love with that song. My love grew deeper when I heard John Denver sing it on the *Doris Day Show*. In appearance and vocal timber, John and I are very similar but his music inspired me not because we share some superficial qualities but because I saw, I heard, and I felt something deeper not only in the man and his music but more importantly in what was behind the music, or what I love to think of as the "super-intention behind the words and the music."

From this, somehow I knew I would go on to write my own songs and with that song as my inspiration, I taught myself to play the guitar. This was a beautiful and transitional time in my life as I renewed my faith in the Lord Jesus Christ. My mom had just remarried and it was difficult as I didn't get along well with my new stepdad. We had just moved down the street and it was spring time (my favorite time of year) and I was truly born again just like John wrote in his autobiographical song "Rocky Mountain High." When I listened to "Rocky Mountain High" the first time in my bedroom at 13 years old I began to sing to the record. This song strikes a deep and resonant chord within me each and every time I hear it or sing it. It captures the essence of something deeper. As an artist, life comes to you in images. In life one has mostly fleeting moments when one is sure, and many more when one is not so sure about one's calling...

During our conversation that fateful day when Mary Fisher Diaz told me that she liked my song "Coming Home" better than any John Denver song, I cried. My reaction wasn't about Mary's sweet compliment or the favorable comparison to John Denver whose music fills my heart and Mary's heart and the hearts of people all around the world. I was moved by this seemingly fortuitous fellowship of mutual understanding of the meaning behind the song, and really, the meaning behind our very existence! That was the essence of the conversation. That sweet ephemeral secret we all carry with us deep in our hearts as it nurtures us through the joys and sorrows of life and on rare occasions finds expression and release through music. A resolution of the tension of life itself, peace...a point where words become utterly superfluous...this inexpressibly sweet and powerful eternal longing for home. C.S Lewis says that when we have a longing this world cannot satisfy that means we were made for another world.

Mary and I talked about this as we shared a brief moment on the phone singing, talking, praying, and even laughing. She expressed the deep love of her family, Isabella, and the love her life, Carlos... The best that my words can summon of the idea of that brief and shining moment is that it was a holy moment. There was this sense that she somehow knew she was coming home and there was no turning back. Finality without fear. Peace. Fellowship and communion with the Spirit of God in our final moments as we become aware of them. I just wish I could express how grateful I am for the privilege of this phone call which I consider to be one of the greatest gifts God has given me in my life. I had this feeling that Mary connected with and understood my own song and the meaning behind it better than I did. And when her time came, the music of Heaven gently seized her heart and welcomed her Home. Peace.

Thank you dear Mary! I will carry this memory in my voice and my heart each and every time I sing your song!

> *Surely goodness and mercy shall follow me all the days of my life: and I will dwell in the house of the Lord for ever.*
>
> *Psalm 23:6*

Peace, Rick Schuler

Here are the lyrics to the title track of Rick's most recent CD Coming Home, dedicated to Mary Fisher Diaz.

— ॐ —

COMING HOME

Copyright © 2014. Words and music by Rick Schuler.

Yesterday …On the plane back home
A thought occurred to me…
What if…
I never…Would see your smile again
To hold you… To love you…
To have you near me…
Suddenly tears…Sliding down my face
Darlin', I missed you so…I never want to let you go
(Chorus)
Coming home is to see your smile
To hold you close to me
To feel your love
Coming home to you
Is to never say goodbye
I'm looking out my window…As we begin to land
Stepped off my plane and made my way through
the crowd
Longing…. to find you…in a sea of faces

My eyes ahead of me racing to find your smile
Darlin' I missed you so... I never want to
let you go

(Chorus)

Suddenly I'm holding on too tightly
So suddenly I'm letting go...
In that day, when I'll be home
Finally to see your smiling face
And feel your loving arms surrounding me
I'll soon be coming home...
No more tears... No more letting go...
No more goodbyes
My darlin' I'll see your smile again
My soul longs for home
My soul longs for home
My soul longs for home
I'll soon be coming home...

— ❦ —

I just have to add that Rick Schuler is one of my most gentle and caring friends. His love and singing have helped me make it through many of the hardest times in my life. He has added so much sunshine to my life. *Love you like crazy Rick!*

Be sure to listen to your free CD that came with this book.

ABOUT *THE AUTHOR*

Writing has always been a passion of Barbara Jeanne Fisher. It has been said that whenever something inspired her that she thought might make a good story, she would grab a napkin from a table to write some words down! She has written two children's books, two novels, along with hundreds of articles for magazines in the United States and Canada.

Her newest book, *Until We Meet Again,* was written after her eldest daughter passed away from stage IV cancer. She said that writing this has been therapeutic. "The pain from losing Mary will always be here in my heart, but it has helped with accepting this sadness.

The biggest reason for writing this book is to share what Mary's death has taught me:

If you feel something is wrong, do not wait to go to the doctor and have all the needed tests. Some doctors have told me that if Mary had had the tests earlier it might not have made a difference because her cancer was fast growing. But, even if only a little chance, there was a chance that it might have changed the ending of this story.

Please, I stress, do not wait, always put yourself first. You only get one life.

WA